STEAM COLOUR PORTFOLIO

Isle of Man Railway Part 1

Compiled by Tom Sherratt

Keith R. Pirt

BOOK LAW PUBLICATIONS

There are two very different ways of arriving on the Isle of Man, by sea or by air. The Isle of Man Steam Packet Co. steamer LADY OF MANN is berthed at Douglas Harbour bathed by the sun of a July evening in 1957. The vessel was built in 1930 at the Vickers Armstrong shipyard at Barrow in Furness. *BLP – C953*.

First published in the United Kingdom by Book Law Publications 2009
382 Carlton Hill, Nottingham, NG4 1JA
Printed and bound by The Amadeus Press, Cleckheaton, West Yorkshire

INTRODUCTION

This book is not a history of the Isle of Man Railway. For that you can do no better than consult the histories of the railway by the late James l. C. Boyd. The detail and knowledge of the Boyd volumes is exact and in very great depth.

I was first attracted to the work of Keith Pirt when Book Law published its first two full colour albums of Keith's work. The quality is without doubt the finest ever produced, since then there have been several volumes, with a promise of more to come.

It is therefore a great privilege to be asked to put together this glorious collection of images of the Isle of Man Railway. You will notice that most photos are taken in bright sunshine, from my knowledge of weather in the Isle of Man this is nothing short of a miracle.

The intention in this first of two volumes is to capture the state of the railway during the company period, all of the pictures date from 1957 to 1963. The second volume will feature the railway over those same dates, besides the years of 1967 and 1968 in what is known as the Ailsa period. Not every area of the Isle of Man railway system is covered, principally because access to certain locations was actively discouraged at this time. However I hope that this will be forgiven and the results deemed to be worthwhile.

During the period of the Isle of Man Railway history a total of sixteen steam locomotives existed and eleven of those are pictured here along with my favourites, the former County Donegal railcars Nos.19 and 20, both built in Wigan, part of the Borough in which I live. Four steam locomotives were in store, in various dismantled forms, but they did exist. They were No.2 DERBY, No.4 LOCH, No.7 TYNWALD and No.9 DOUGLAS. Engine No.15 CALEDONIA, a former Manx Northern locomotive, was also in reserve, fitted with snow ploughs.

The Isle of Man is a wonderful place which I first visited in 1962 and then almost every year since 1971. I have met many Manx people, some alas no longer with us. Their friendship knew no bounds and if you have not been to the island, I would respectfully suggest that you make the effort to go - you will not be disappointed - if only for the trains, trams and buses. Travelling on a double-decker bus around rural parts of the island is an attraction in itself.

However the Island has a lot to offer visitors and there is much more to see and admire. Oh and don't forget to say hello to the fairies whilst you are there!!

Tom Sherratt, Lowton, September 2009

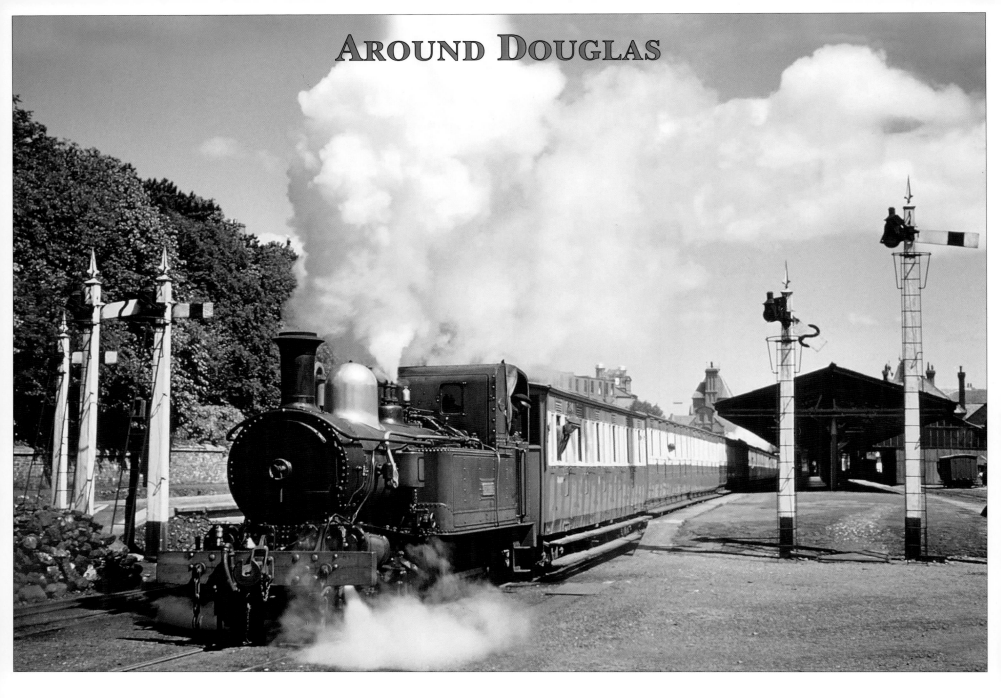

Built in 1905 and named after a former manager and director of the company, engine No.10 G.H.WOOD is departing from Douglas in charge of a heavy afternoon train to Port Erin in May 1957. An unknown banker adds support at the rear of the train. *BLP – C122*.

A classic view of No.14 THORNHILL, taken in the bay platform next to the goods yard with the goods shed on the right. The train is about to pull out its carriage stock and set back into the Port Erin platform to the left to leave for the south in May 1957. Note No.14's original Salter values. *BLP – C121*.

The first locomotive built for the Isle of Man Railway in 1873, No.1 SUTHERLAND - named after the Duke of Sutherland, the first chairman of the company. No.1 has just brought in a train from Ramsey and is seen at the throat of Douglas station in June 1962. Before returning with a passenger service to Ramsey – where it was usually kept – the locomotive is about to be serviced near the shed. Snow plough at the ready in June! *BLP – C88*.

No.13 KISSACK, built in 1910, awaits its turn of duty at Douglas on a sunny afternoon in July 1957. KISSACK was named after another director of the company. The locomotive stands just below Railway Terrace - a good viewing platform when the trees are not in leaf. *BLP – C161.*

No.3 PENDER, built in 1873, gets ready at Douglas for an afternoon service in July 1957 to a sunny destination. *BLP – C123*.

No.16 MANNIN with a late afternoon service to Port Erin pulls quickly away from Douglas, in readiness to climb up though the Nunnery cutting and Port Soderick bank in July 1957. *BLP – C162*.

During May 1962, No.10 G.H.WOOD stands at Douglas coal dock - situated at the throat of the station - taking a rest before its next turn of duty possibly to Peel and Ramsey, the train splitting at St Johns. *BLP – C167*.

This locomotive looks the same but it is not. No.11 MAITLAND, built in 1905, at Douglas May 1963 in the exact same spot as No.10 in the previous illustration. What more needs to be said except that this engine followed Company practice and was named after a Director of the enterprise. *BLP – C168.*

No.13 KISSACK leaves Douglas with a train to Ramsey in May 1962. Above the locomotive is Railway Terrace from where a panoramic view of the station can be seen, when the trees are not in leaf. During the early morning when the engines are being prepared for work, Railway Terrace becomes quite thick with smoke. *BLP – C166.*

What a magnificent sight! Nos.6 PEVERIL and 3 PENDER await their afternoon train duties at the north side of Douglas station in July 1957. It looks a blustery but very bright day. *BLP – C222*.

No.8 FENELLA stands by the coal loading dock at Douglas Locomotive Shed ready for its next turn of duty in June 1963. *BLP – C208.*

Ready for the off at Douglas in July 1962, double-headed train for Peel and Ramsey has No.12 HUTCHINSON and No 8 FENELLA in charge. The train will divide at St Johns. *BLP – C444.*

Waiting for its next turn of duty, No.10 G.H.WOOD stands on the shed road on the north side of Douglas station in July 1957. *BLP – C388.*

No.3 PENDER stands on the shed access line at Douglas station with empty coaching stock behind. A train to Peel and Ramsey is waiting at the platform under the station roof in May 1957. *BLP – C391*.

No.10 G.H.WOOD departs from the Peel and Ramsey arrival platform of Douglas station with a late afternoon train to Peel in July 1957. Note that the station building in the background is the Head Office of the railway company. *BLP – C401*.

Full coal baskets can be seen as No.1 SUTHERLAND awaits servicing in the coal road at Douglas station. Although the photograph was taken in July 1962 the locomotive still sports its snow plough. *BLP – C803.*

A sideways view of No.8 FENELLA awaiting departure for Peel in July 1963. *BLP – C801.*

Appearing to create the clouds in an otherwise clear sky, No.10 G.H.WOOD awaits departure at Douglas with a heavy morning train to Port Erin in July 1963. The train will be banked at the rear. *BLP – C820*.

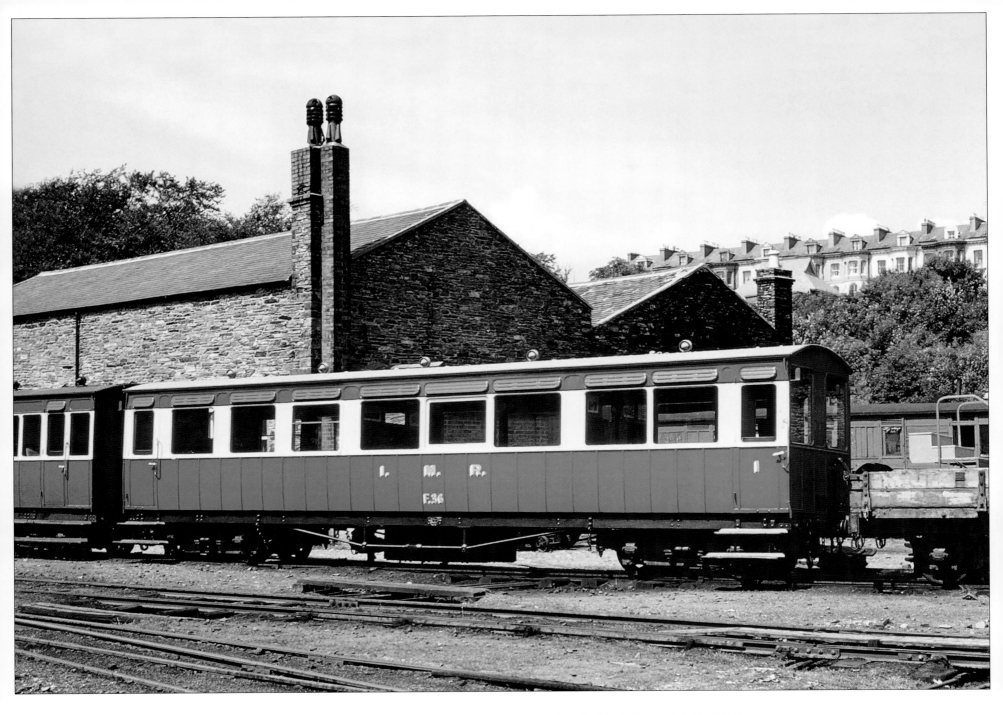

Isle of Man Railway Saloon coach F36, just ex-works, stands on the line alongside Douglas locomotive shed in July 1963. *BLP – C961.*

Isle of Man Railway Brake coach F41 is the brake vehicle on a Ramsey line train in Douglas station in July 1963. *BLP – C962*.

General opinion has it that Union Mills was the most attractive station on the railway. No.10 G.H.WOOD approaches at a sedate pace with a train for Peel and Ramsey in July 1957. Note the platform on the right covered with rhododendron bushes having just lost there flower - in May and June a magnificent sight. *BLP – C124*.

With a line of conifer trees to the left giving the whole scene some scale, colour and style, No.13 KISSACK nears Union Mills station with a Douglas to Peel and Ramsey train in July 1957. Note the all clear home signal in the background. *BLP – C182.*

No.5 MONA crosses the River Dhoo bridge before entering Union Mills station with an afternoon Douglas to Peel service in May 1957. *BLP – C1065*.

Seen heading for Douglas, No.14 THORNHILL is at St Johns in May 1957. Built in 1880 for the former Manx Northern Railway, it was the only Beyer Peacock locomotive supplied to that line. Fitted with Salter valves, the engine was merged into the Isle of Man Railway Co fleet in the 1905 amalgamation. Currently privately preserved on the island and was named after the residence of the first chairman of the Manx Northern Railway Co. *BLP – C71*.

Locomotive No.5 MONA, built in 1874 and wearing Indian red livery, arrives at St Johns with an afternoon service from Douglas to Peel in May 1957. St Johns is the home of Tynwald the island's parliament and was a junction with lines from Douglas, Peel and Ramsey. The abandoned line to Foxdale, which tapped into minerals extracted from the mines in that area, and which closed to passengers in 1939, created an additional junction here. Tynwald Day (5th July) in the life of a Manx resident is a very important occasion which stretched the railway services to their limit in the past. *BLP – C65.*

The steam race is on in May 1957 with No.8 FENELLA, built in 1894 (1eft), on a Ramsey train and No.14 THORNHILL (right) on a train for Peel. The scene was captured early afternoon with a split train from Douglas departing St Johns at the same time - a classic image that was more down to luck rather than being the norm. It has been known for this type of shot to be stage managed but this scene did happen by talking to Mr Crellin the St Johns Station Master. *BLP – C118.*

No.14 THORNHILL arrives at St Johns with a split train from Douglas to Peel and Ramsey. In July 1957 the train stops at this point and Thornhill pulls forward with the Peel portion into the south loop. A light locomotive will come forward to haul the Ramsey portion into the north loop. To the left is the carriage shed and in the distance, behind the train, is the arch bridge which carried the line into Foxdale. The line would still be in situ but derelict. Note the advertisement hoardings boards to the right. This was in a good location whilst all the manoeuvring of trains took place. *BLP – C156*.

Another shot in May 1962 of No.5 MONA on a Peel to Douglas train at St Johns. Built in 1874, the locomotive is ready to couple up with the portion from Ramsey before departure. *BLP – C165*.

No.8 FENELLA having collected its train (see page 30) is waiting to leave for Ramsey in the northern loop - there was no race this day. Note the advertising hoardings to the left with amongst them Kodak and beer adverts. It all adds to the atmosphere at St Johns in July 1957. In the distance, signal box, water tank and carriage sheds can be seen. *BLP – C159.*

County Donegal railcars Nos.19 and 20, coupled back to back, arrive at St Johns with a Douglas - Peel service. Not only were these railcars saved for posterity in the 1960's by the Isle of Man Railway Co., but provided a useful addition to the rolling stock. Both railcars were built in my home Borough of Wigan at Walker Brothers built originally in 1950 for the County Donegal Railway in Ireland. They arrived on the island in May 1961 and are seen here in service during May 1962. *BLP – C164*.

St Johns station in July 1962 with No.13 KISSACK heading a Ramsey train consisting two goods vans in the formation. A Douglas bound train is at the rear. *BLP – C966.*

Having traversed the road crossing at St Johns, No.12 HUTCHINSON is on its way to Ramsey in June 1963. You will note that there is not a train for Peel in sight – once again, no race today. No.12 is approaching the junction of the closed Foxdale line. Stood near the road crossing from St Johns to Foxdale is George Crellin the St Johns Station Master, and getting ready to open the level crossing gates is Mrs. Crellin. *BLP – C171*.

In May 1962 No.5 MONA is on its way to Peel having just left St Johns. On the embankment in the distance climbs the Ramsey line towards the overbridge which takes the Douglas to Peel Road under the line. *BLP – C184.*

A very busy day at St Johns - waiting for the off in July 1957. No.8 FENELLA (left) heads a Ramsey mixed train and No.14 THORNHILL waits to the right with a Peel train. On No.8's left hand side stands a train from Ramsey/Peel to Douglas. *BLP – C223.*

In a sylvan setting at St Johns - change here for Ramsey - No.14 THORNHILL awaits the right away for a Douglas to Peel train in July 1957. *BLP – C281.*

No.13 KISSACK just arrived at St Johns with a train from Peel in June 1962. This train, and another one due to arrive from Ramsey, will couple together to form a service to Douglas. *BLP – C275.*

The rear aspect of County Donegal railcar set Nos.19 and 20 in June 1962 as they approach St Johns station (to the right) on a service from Peel to Douglas. In the left hand distance the line from Ramsey comes in to join the Peel line on the straight approach to the station. *BLP – C274.*

No.16 MANNIN, standing at St Johns in July 1963. Again on arrival from Peel, just to prove the point that such a large loco is not only for the South Line. At this time the boiler is weak and life expired. *BLP – C282*.

No.10 G.H.WOOD gets away from St Johns in May 1957 with a Douglas to Ramsey train. Note the abandoned cattle wagons in the sidings and the old Foxdale line station to the left centre. *BLP – C390.*

No.12 HUTCHINSON runs forward with a mixed train to Ramsey at St Johns in June 1963. Note the guard on the coach running board during the splitting operation of the Douglas train to Peel and Ramsey. To the left is the carriage shed. *BLP – C496.*

No.14 THORNHILL has come to a halt at the eastern end of St Johns under the Foxdale line bridge with an early afternoon train to Peel and Ramsey. The guard has got off the train ready to split its formation of coaches to form the two trains in St Johns station. A spare locomotive will be waiting to take on the Ramsey portion in the station loop. *BLP – C584.*

No.13 KISSACK rests by the water tower at St Johns. A bogie luggage van, F27 which was supplied in 1897, stands behind the locomotive in June 1957. *BLP – C805.*

The disused locomotive turntable at St Johns in May 1957, with a line of abandoned wagons occupying the sidings beyond. Identified by their numbers are wagons M4 and M41, which are near the shed. Also visible is the disused mineral line to Foxdale. *BLP – C807.*

No.8 FENELLA, with a Douglas to Peel train, awaits departure from St Johns station in July 1963. *BLP – C882*.

In July 1963, No.8 FENELLA propels coaches into St Johns station. The red board attached to the bufferbeam indicates "Special following in opposite direction". These usually appeared on the Sunday service specials from Douglas to Kirk Braddan. *BLP – C963*.

No.12 HUTCHINSON (built in 1908) awaiting departure from Peel in June 1963 with a service to St Johns and Douglas. The late afternoon sun creates a splendid sight. *BLP – C169.*

A spectacular view of Peel as seen from Corrin's Hill in July 1957. With the station and harbour also in frame, Peel, known as the sunset city, glows in the bright summer sunlight of July 1957. What a lovely coast line on the west of the island, looking north towards the Ayres. *BLP – C346*.

Ex County Donegal railcars Nos.19 and 20, coupled back to back, are taking on passengers at Peel station in June 1962. In the far left background is Peel castle overlooking the harbour. *BLP – C319*.

Stood on the shed road at Peel station is No.5 MONA in May 1957. The area usually had the smell of Manx Kippers being cured and packed to send to all parts of the British Isles by post from the Isle of Man as part of its trade. *BLP – C389.*

A long distance view of Peel station and harbour in July 1963. In the station No.8 FENELLA heads a four coach train to Douglas. Note the Viking boat grounded by the low tide against the harbour wall. *BLP – C802*.

No.8 FENELLA waits departure from Peel bay platform with a Douglas train in July 1963. *BLP – C446*.

No.5 MONA outside the locomotive shed at Peel in May 1957. A roofless wooden shed has been erected in front of a roofed stone shed. The stone shed remains intact to the present day. Peel station is now the House of Manannan, a museum of Manx life, opened in 1997. *BLP – C806*.

Our cover picture on the west coast of the island has some magnificent scenery with No.5 MONA heading a train to Ramsey whilst skirting the Irish Sea at Gob y-Deigan in June 1962. Sometimes you can just see the headland of Peel in the distance as the train forges towards Kirk Michael, its next stop. On the way two major viaducts – the only such structures on the island – at Glen Mooar and Glen Wyllin will be traversed. *BLP – C96*.

No.12 HUTCHINSON now crosses the Glen Mooar Viaduct en route to Ramsey in June 1963. The view, looking towards the sea, is on the west coast of the island. Shortly the train will cross Glen Wyllin viaduct, below which was Glen Wyllin park, a good spot to see trains arriving and departing Kirk Michael station. *BLP – C172*.

Railcars Nos.19 and 20 have just crossed the Glen Mooar viaduct - next stop Kirk Michael - on a Douglas to Ramsey working in July 1963. *BLP – C445*.

No.12 HUTCHINSON leaves Kirk Michael with an exceptionally long Douglas to Ramsey train in June 1963. All the station buildings on the Northern line, from St Johns to Ramsey, were built in stone with one exception - Peel Road a small timber-built wayside halt. *BLP – C500*.

No.12 HUTCHINSON puts up a smoke screen climbing the bank out of Douglas with a morning mixed train to Port Erin in May 1957. On the Isle of Man Railway trains ran mixed with goods vans or wagons attached to the rear of the passenger vehicles. *BLP – C224.*

With an early morning train, the work horse of the South Line, No.16 MANNIN, ascends the bank towards Port Soderick in May 1963. Although only lightly loaded with just four bogies, the train was somewhat 'large' for so early in the season. *BLP – C117.*

No.16 MANNIN has just entered Oakhill cutting under the road bridge with a Douglas to Port Erin train in May 1957. *BLP – C400.*

On a glorious summer afternoon in July 1957, No.16 MANNIN rounds the curve south of Santon with what appears to be a Douglas to Port Erin mixed train with five saloon stock coaches in the formation. *BLP – C181*.

Without any effort at all No.12 HUTCHINSON climbs Oakhill bank with a Douglas to Port Erin train in June 1963. Added to this, is the wonderful view of the foot hills of Snaefell. *BLP – C499*.

In May 1957 No.10 G.H.WOOD approaches Santon, along the vegetation strewn permanent way, with an afternoon Douglas to Port Erin train. Note the signal in the off position in the distance. *BLP – C318*.

No.16 MANNIN works a Port Erin to Douglas train past the old signal on the approach to Santon in July 1957. *BLP – C965.*

No.16 MANNIN, the last locomotive built for the railway in 1926, was a much stronger version of the Beyer Peacock locomotives on the island. The principal reason for its existence was for the heavy South Line trains to Port Erin. No.16 is climbing through the summit cutting in May 1957 with a rather heavy train for so early in the season. Note the track is almost covered with vegetation. *BLP – C72.*

No.12 HUTCHINSON arriving at Ballasalla with a late afternoon Douglas to Port Erin train in July 1957. Alight here for Rushen Abbey - it was also the local station for the islands airport, but a fair walk at that. *BLP C234.*

With plenty of steam to spare, No.16 MANNIN leaves Ballasalla with a Douglas to Port Erin train in July 1963. *BLP – C441*.

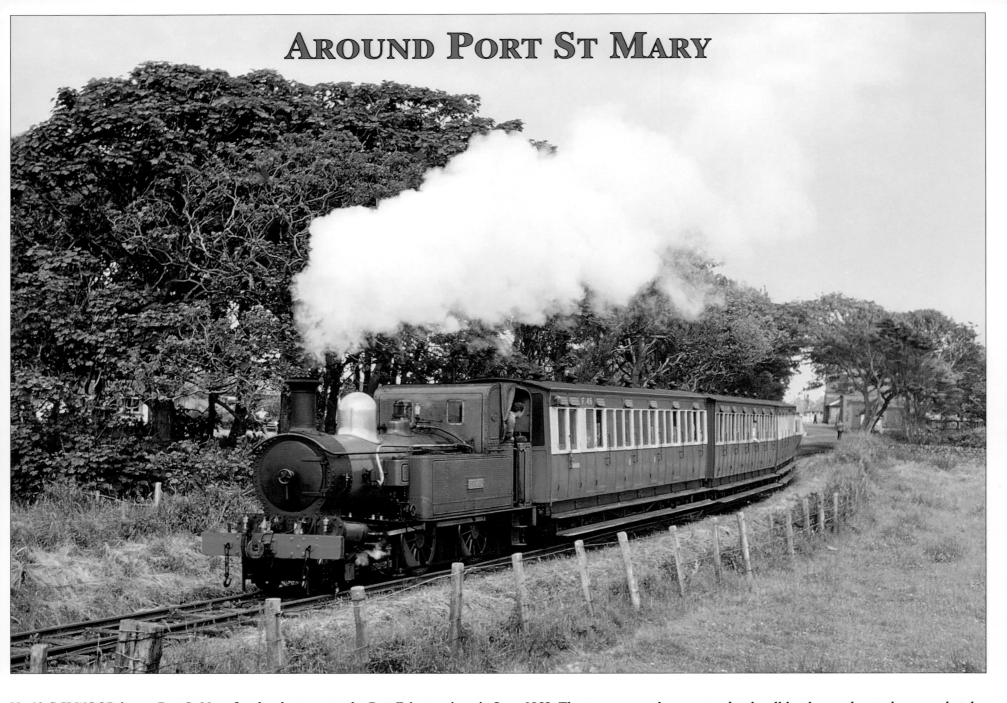

No.10 G.H.WOOD leaves Port St Mary for the short run to the Port Erin terminus in June 1963. The trees, as can be seen, tend to be all but brown due to the somewhat dry weather. *BLP – C170*.

No.16 MANNIN, with steam to spare, at Port St Mary station in June 1963 - next stop Port Erin terminus of the line. Note the different condition of the engine to that depicted on page 41. *BLP – C348*.

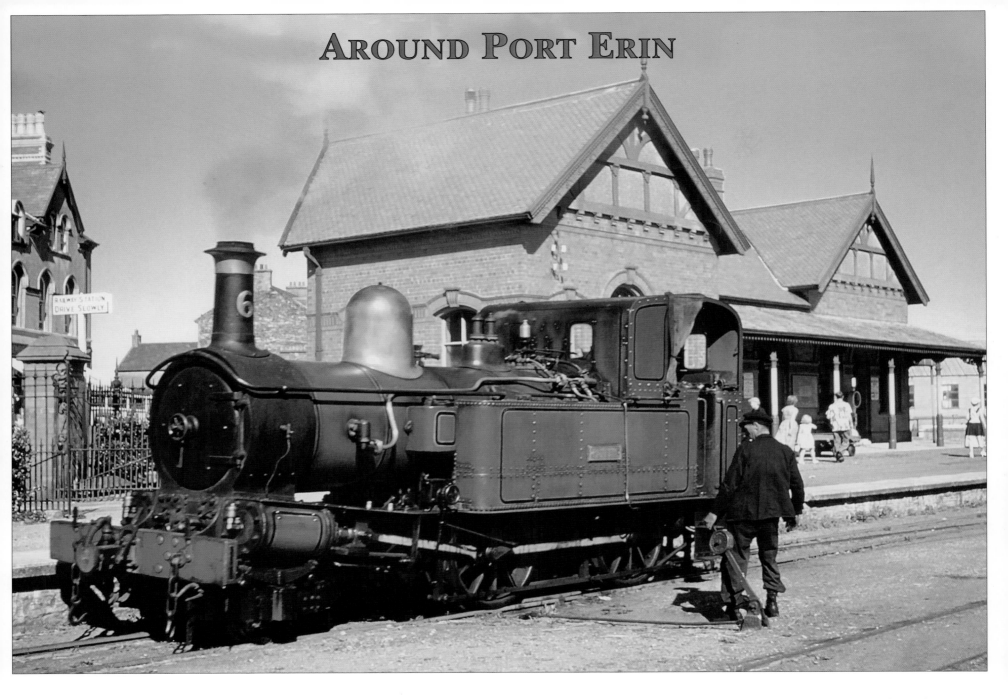

A classic Port Erin view of No.6 PEVERIL, built in 1875, running round its train to have a rest after servicing at the shed prior to returning to Douglas. Port Erin Station was one of the largest stations on the line and the classic red brick gives real warmth even in the bright sunshine of July 1957. *BLP – C157.*

No.16 MANNIN arrives in the bay platform at Port Erin with a train from Douglas in July 1957. Port Erin station was unusual in the fact that it had a public footpath running across the line which effectively cut the platform in two. *BLP – C225.*

No.10 G.H.WOOD reverses at Port Erin station to run round its train and enter the locomotive shed road for coaling and watering ready for the next return service back to Douglas in July 1963. *BLP – C273.*

No.6 PEVERIL having been serviced at Port Erin gets ready to couple up to its return working to Douglas. This train could be heavy indeed taking day tripper's back to Douglas or to the steamer going to Fleetwood or Llandudno. *BLP – C253*.

In what is a good view from the buffer stops at the southern terminus, No.6 PEVERIL runs round its train at Port Erin in July 1957. It is likely that the locomotive will run into the shed road on the right for servicing before heading back to Douglas. The station is to the left of the locomotive. *BLP – C316.*

No.11 MAITLAND arrives at Port Eirn with an afternoon train in July 1963. *BLP – C442*.

No.10 G. H. WOOD arrives at Port Erin with a train from Douglas in July 1963. *BLP – C580.*

Running into Port Erin station is No.6 PEVERIL with a mixed train from Douglas. Coach F33 and a low wagon in the bay platform all make an attractive scene in July 1957. *BLP – C1066.*

We end this album where we will start off the next. No.11 MAITLAND passes No.5 MONA outside Douglas station whilst working a late afternoon Douglas to Port Erin service in July 1967. *BLP – C239.*